Words

© 2015 OnBoard Academics, Inc
Portsmouth, NH
800-596-3175
www.onboardacademics.com
ISBN: 978-1-63096-037-7

OnBoard Academic's books are specifically designed to be used as printed workbooks or as on-screen instruction. Each page offers focused exercises and students quickly master topics with enough proficiency to move on to the next level.

OnBoard Academic's lessons are used in over 25,000 classrooms to rave reviews. Our lessons are aligned to the most recent governmental standards and are updated from time to time as standards change. Correlation documents are located on our website. Our lessons are created, edited and evaluated by educators to ensure top quality and real life success.

Interactive lessons for digital whiteboards, mobile devices, and PCs are available at www.onboardacademics.com. These interactive lessons make great additions to our books.

You can always reach us at customerservice@onboardacademics.com.

Multiple Meanings

Key Vocabulary

verb

noun

context

context clues

Multiple Meanings

Which image illustrates the word light?

We should light the fire soon.

Can you turn on the light?

> **A multiple meaning word is a word that has more than one meaning depending on how it is used in a sentence.**

Noun vs. Verb

> noun

There was still a drop of coffee left,

> verb

so I was careful not to drop the mug.

> **Understanding if the word is used as a noun or verb can help you to determine its meaning.**

Identify the correct definition (√) for the multiple meaning word.

The class is taking a trip to see a play.
- [ ] to engage with for fun (v)
- [ ] to take part in (v)
- [ ] a dramatic performance (n)

The hunters followed the coyote tracks.
- [ ] a course laid out for running or racing (n)
- [ ] to follow a course (v)
- [ ] marks left by something (n)

The snap on Mia's purse is broken.
- [ ] to make a sharp cracking sound (v)
- [ ] the release of something under pressure (n)
- [ ] a fastening device (n)

Identify the multiple meaning word and its type.

Fill in the blanks and identify if the multiple meaning word is a noun (N), or a verb(V).

☐ My dad picked up a can of ☐ on his way home.

☐ He was going to ☐ that squeaky door hinge.

☐ We made sure to ☐ the envelope tightly.

☐ Then we attached the family ☐ to the evelope.

☐ There was a loud ☐ in the other room.

☐ Brian had broken a vase with his tennis ☐ .

(N) (V)   oil   seal   racket

Context Clues

> Using *context clues* can help you identify the correct definition for a multiple meaning word.

information in the text

The river ***bank*** was muddy from the rain.

what you already know

We had to get money at the ***bank***.

Use contact clues to match the picture card with the sentence. You can match by drawing a line.

 Tori will watch for any unfamiliar faces.

 Brian put his father's watch on his wrist.

 We saw the turn sign up ahead.

 I had to sign the check so I could deposit it.

Use context clues to match the sentences with the correct multiple meaning word definition.

There is a recall on spinach.

I can't recall when we were last at gramma's house.

I can carry both boxes.

Will you grab the can of beans for me?

Her hands were rough from hard labor.

The boy gave a hand hoisting the flag.

part of the body

indicates physical ability

the act of taking back

the ability to remember

help or assistance

a metal container

Name:

Multiple Meanings Quiz

1. In this sentence, the word break is used as a verb: Let's take a break. True or false?

2. Which is not the meaning for the word trade?
   a. to switch
   b. a skill
   c. to fight
   d. none of the above

3. In which sentence is the word track used as a noun?
   a. Stay safely away from the train track.
   b. Did you track down the person you were looking for?
   c. The meteorologist likes to track weather patterns.
   d. none of the above

4. In which sentence is the word mean used as a noun?
   a. Don't be so mean to your brother.
   b. The mean of 3, 4, and 5 is 4.
   c. I didn't mean to offend you.
   d. all of the above

Idioms

Key Vocabulary

idioms

similes

metaphors

What does kick the bucket mean?

"Nibbles, my hamster, has kicked the bucket."

☐ Nibbles has kicked a bucket

☐ Nibbles has died

☐ Nibbles has made a sandcastle

Similes, Metaphors and Idioms

s | "Fernando is as cunning as a fox."
Similes compare two unlike things typically using the words *like* or *as*.

m | "James is a busy beaver."
In a metaphor, one thing (James) is said to be another thing (a beaver).

i | "David has a chip on his shoulder."
Idioms are like irregular metaphors; they are widely understood, but often defy literal translation.

Context Clues and Idioms

Use context clues to find the meanings of these idioms. Write the idiom in the proper box and then define it below.

After she had gone through all of the steps, the math

teacher said, "That's all you need to know about division

[   ]".

"Even if we don't do the test tomorow, you'll need to know

your division facts [   ] for the next lesson."

I was [   ] when I took the test, because I'd

forgotten all of my division facts!

| in a jam | in a nutshell | in any case |

Idioms

Which word or phrase is closest in meaning to each idiom?

in a nutshell	
in any case	
in a jam	

in some difficulty   without a doubt   most definitely

short summary   my opinion   regardless

Select the correct definition for each idiom.

James thinks his dad is out of touch.		never cuddles him doesn't understand
We couldn't agree so Tori left in a huff.		feeling angry new wool coat
Owen went out on a limb to get the ball off of the roof.		took a risk hurt his arm
When we saw signs for our hometown we knew we were over the hump.		traveled by camel worst is over
When she heard the news here reaction was over the top.		excessive too high pitched

Match the blue cards with the correct idiom.

having a ball	cut it out	feeling blue

green thumb	stood by	crack up

sad	good gardener	a great time
watched and did nothing	laugh	stop it

www.onboardacademics.com

Name_____

Idioms Quiz

1. If a test is a piece of cake, it will be hard. True or false?

2. Dad's new car cost an arm and a leg.
   a. hardly anything
   b. he paid in body parts
   c. a lot of money
   d. it was free

3. After the big game, I chowed down the burritos.
   a. cooked
   b. discarded
   c. saw
   d. ate

4. Bob nearly jumped out of his skin when he heard a loud crash of thunder.
   a. got excited
   b. got soaking wet
   c. was amazed
   d. was surprised

Synonyms and Antonyms

Key Vocabulary

synonyms

antonyms

Replace the Word

Replace the word enormous with three other words that mean the same thing.

This dinosaur is | enormous | !

This dinosaur is | | !

This dinosaur is | | !

This dinosaur is | | !

These words are *synonyms* for the word enormous. Synonyms are words that have the same or a similar meaning.

Match each word with a synonym.

shrink   pointless   magnify
break   cry   wrong   repair

word	synonym
fix	
weep	
mistaken	
futile	
enlarge	

Order these synonyms by their degree of meaning.

Degree of meaning refers to how strongly the synonym expresses a feeling or an idea. For example, *furious* is a stronger expression of anger than *annoyed*.

Ecstatic

Glad

Delighted

Happy

Overjoyed

Content

    www.onboardacademics.com

Use synonyms to spice up this text!

Rose [said] that her brother Tom

had been very [rude] to her friends.

Rose's Mom was [angry] . "I will not

[allow] that kind of behavior, Tom,"

she said. Tom was [sad] and

[went] upstairs to his bedroom.

Rose [_____] that her brother Tom

had been very [_____] to her friends.

Rose's Mom was [_____] . "I will not

[_____] that kind of behavior, Tom,"

she said. Tom was [_____] and

[_____] upstairs to his bedroom.

Synonyms and Antonyms

Words with similar meanings

Words with opposite meanings

Word	Synonym	Antonym
Rich	Wealthy	Poor

Find synonyms and antonyms.

Word	Synonym	Antonym
Happy		
Sharp		
Important		
Accurate		
Funny		
Exciting		

Pointed	Humorous	Precise	Dreary
Stimulating	Significant	Sad	Cheerful
Dull	Irrelevant	Blunt	Flawed

Synonym and Antonym Quiz

1. Synonyms are words with opposite meanings. True or false?

2. Find the antonym for the word devastated.
    a. distant
    b. sad
    c. delighted
    d. worried

3. Which word is not a synonym of cold?
    a. chilly
    b. calm
    c. cool
    d. crisp

4. Find the antonym for the word slowly.
    a. gradually
    b. never
    c. sometimes
    d. instantly

5. What is an antonym for the word responsible?

    _____

Homonyms

Key Vocabulary

homonym

www.onboardacademics.com

Homonyms,
Spell and say each word.

not daughter

 www.onboardacademics.com

Match the homonym with the definition.

1	An aroma	☐
2	A carnival with rides	☐
3	A fruit	☐
4	Uncomfortably cool	☐
5	A wild pig	☐
6	A chopping tool	☐
7	To hesitate	☐

cent	scent
fare	fair
pause	paws
ax	acts
bore	boar
pair	pear
chilly	chili

Complete the sentence with the correct homonym.
Write the matching homonym in the box.

Did Mom _____ that button on?

It is your turn, _____ the dice.

My dog has a red _____.

The dog was stung by a _____.

Identify the correct homonym pairs.
√ for yes and X for no.

ate	eight	
deer	dear	
ball	bawl	
tore	tour	
soar	sour	
to	two	

_____

Fill in the blank using the correct homonym.

 James could not find a _____ of socks.

 Allan wants to _____ the turkey.

 Anthony gathered some _____ for a fire.

 Ice cream is on _____ five at the grocery store.

The _____ fan whirred quietly.

pair	baste	wood	ceiling	isle
pear	based	would	sealing	aisle

Complete the homonym crossword puzzle.

ACROSS

1. To remove water from a boat.

2. You eat this with milk for breakfast.

3. Garments.

4. Failing to win

5. A small room.

DOWN

1. A bundle of hay.

2. Numbers in sequence.

3. To shut.

4. The opposite of tight.

5. To exchange something for money.

Rhyming Words

Key Vocabulary

rhyme

rhyming words

What do these words have in common?

| clock | lock | sock |

They are *rhyming* words.

> **Rhyming words have the same ending sound, for example, -ock.** DEFINITION

Find a rhyming color for each picture.
Write the color in the box, use the color if you have it available!

| bed | bean | track | two |

Match the rhyming words.

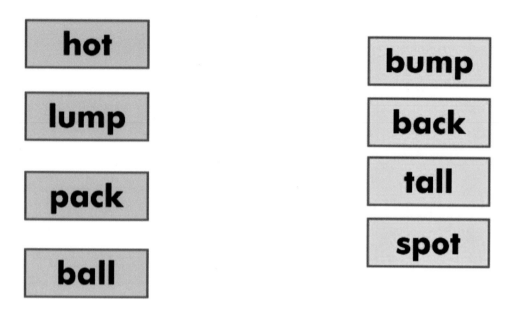

Tic-Tac-Toe

Circle three rhyming words that form tic-tac-toe.

bell	mask	task
trap	well	clap
pet	wet	fell

Fill in the columns with rhyming words.

1	**take**	**bad**	**stop**
2			
3			

List words that rhyme with sing.

				s	i	n	g
					i	n	g
					i	n	g
					i	n	g
					i	n	g

Complete this poem.

Outside my window, I see the glowing moon,

It's late, and I must get to sleep very _____.

I close my book and turn off the bedroom _____,

And call down to my family, "Have a good night!"

Name:

Rhyming Words Quiz

1. Boat rhymes with loaf. True or false?

2. Circle the word that rhymes with ran.
    a. pin
    b. bed
    c. tub
    d. man

3. Circle the word that rhymes with fix.

    a. pit
    b. sit
    c. mix
    d. fin

4. Circle the group of three words that rhyme.

    a. at, lack, ate
    b. bad, sad, sack
    c. dab, crab, grab
    d. man, tan, cap

5. Mug rhymes with cub. True or false?

Homonym Quiz

1. Homonyms are words that sound the same, but are pronounced differently and have different meanings. True or false?

2. Owen has _____ presents to open.
   a. ate
   b. ite
   c. eight
   d. aight

3. The letter was _____ in the mail.
   a. cent
   b. scent
   c. sent

4. The dad held the hand of his _____?
   a. son
   b. sun

5. The little girl turned _____ years old.
   a. to
   b. two
   c. too

6. Don't _____ your new camera.
   a. loose
   b. lose
   c. loss

Homophones

Key Vocabulary

Homophones

www.onboardacademics.com

Match the words.

Write the proper word in the box based on the picture.
After you have filled the boxes, say the words out loud and connect the homophones.

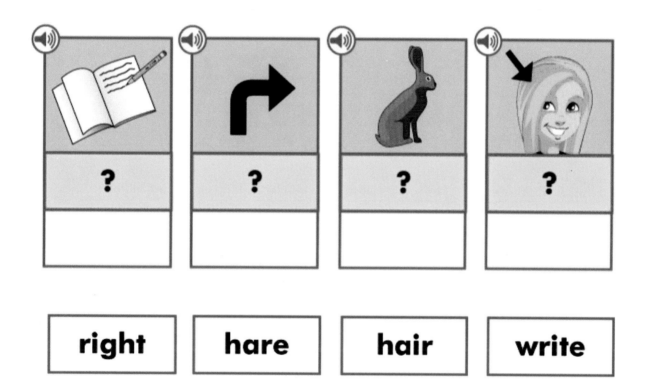

| right | hare | hair | write |

Identify the homophone pairs.

Place a √ next to the pairs of words that are homophones and an X if they are not homophones.

flea	**flew**	
steak	**stake**	
moose	**mousse**	
toe	**tow**	
soar	**sour**	
foul	**fowl**	

www.onboardacademics.com

Complete the pair of homophones.

Bread is made with flour.

A [   ] **is a blossom.**

There are seven days in a week.

[   ] **means not strong.**

We get bargains in a sale.

We [   ] **on the lake in a boat.**

Famous homophones.

Use the proper homophone for each sentences. Your choices are in green below.

They sell books in [   ] bookstore.

My three favorite books are [   ] .

I think that [   ] in the fiction section.

I can't wait to go [   ] !

they're   their   there

Use the clues to identify the proper homophone.
Green suggestions are at the bottom. Write in the proper homophone.

1	Helps to stop a car	
2	People fly in these	
3	A place to go fishing	
4	Slays dragons	
5	It is not polite to do this	

| plane | break | creek | knight | stair |
| brake | plain | creak | night | stare |

Write a homophone in the spaces provided.

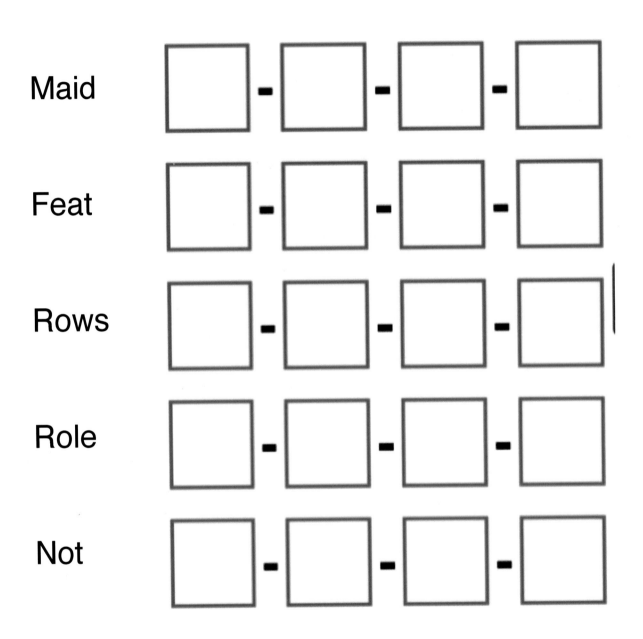

Maid

Feat

Rows

Role

Not

Complete the homophone crossword puzzle.

ACROSS

1. A very strong metal.

2. When your voice is rough or harsh.

3. Single.

4. Mia loves the rides at the State _____.

DOWN

1. To take what isn't yours.

2. Cowboys ride these.

3. When you lend or borrow something.

4. The cost of a ride on the bus.

Name_____

Homophone Quiz

1. True or false? Homophones are words that are spelled the same.

2. Fill in the blank. Rapunzel had very long beautiful _____. HARE HAIR

3. Fill in the blank. I am excited _____ sleep. TO TOU TOO TWO

4. Fill in the blank. The plane _____ over our house. FLU FLEW FEW

5. Fill in the blank. _____ uniforms were blakc and yellow. THERE THEY"RE THEIR

6. Fill in the blank. I found the coin over _____> THERE THEY"RE THEIR

7. Fill in the blank. Which is the _____ answer? WRITE RIGHT RITE

8. Circle the pair of words that are not homophones
   a. FEET, FEAT
   b. BEET, BEAT
   c. HOLE, HAUL
   d. HEARD, HERD

Precise Words

Key Vocabulary

precise word

noun

verb

Precise Words
Put a check mark next to the sentence that uses more precise words. Underline the differences.

Precise words give a more accurate description and tell the reader *exactly* what is happening.

The girl is with the dog.

The girl is walking the black lab.

www.onboardacademics.com

Connect a precise word for each of these nouns.
Connect the noun with the precise word and then the more detailed picture.

> **Precise nouns** are words that describe specific people, places or things.

boy	flower	bird	car
	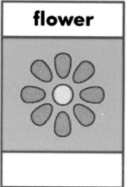		

rose	plover	convertible	Owen

Replace the nouns in red with a precise word by writing it underneath the red noun.

We took the ___boat___ out on the lake.

Brian stepped on a ___bug___.

Use the ___tool___ to put the nail in.

Owen gave Mia some ___flowers___.

Precise Verbs

Precise verbs are words that describe specific actions and can help *show the reader a story* and not just *tell a story*.

Read the two passages. Notice the difference in meaning and detail when precise verbs are used.

David and I had been walking for hours.

We sat under an old maple tree.

I gave him some of my granola bar.

"Look over there," David said.

I saw a big bear in the distance.

David and I had been hiking for hours.

We rested under an old maple tree.

I shared some of my granola bar.

"Look over there," David exclaimed.

I glimpsed a big bear in the distance.

    www.onboardacademics.com

Identify Precise Verbs
Put a check in the box to indicate the sentence uses a precise verb. If the sentence uses a general verb, suggest a precise verb.

James | devoured | his dinner. ☐

The dog | walked | across the lawn. ☐

Grace | tumbled | down the hill ☐

She | put | her paper in the trash. ☐

My dad | cut | the turkey for dinner. ☐

Mia is | filthy | after playing outside. ☐

Name_____

Precise Words Quiz

1. Precise nouns describe specific people, places or things. True or false?

2. Fill in the blank with the most precise noun. Jason held the _____ up to the light. rock sapphire stone gem

3. Fill in the blank with a precise word. The bird _____ in the tree. walked chirped fell was

4. Complete with a precise word. The swimmer _____ across the pool.

5. Circle the most precise verb. tiptoed walked went left

6. Fill in the blank with the most precise word. The diver _____ off the diving board. jumped went got somersaulted

7. Fill in the blank with the most precise word. We finally reached the _____ of the mountain. top end peak high

Made in the USA
Middletown, DE
18 December 2017